ALEXANDER MURRAY;

GALLOWAY'S SELF-TAUGHT GENIUS

by

Jack Hunter

Published by
STRANRAER AND DISTRICT LOCAL HISTORY TRUST

For my family

© JACK HUNTER 2014

ISBN
978-1-906737-10-8

Published by
Stranraer and District Local History Trust
Tall Trees
London Road
Stranraer DG9 8BZ

Charity Number SC 028177

www.stranraerhistory.org.uk

Manor of Urr June 18th 1810

Dear Sir,

I received your esteemed favour respecting the disputed Marches of Corwar and Dunkillerick and shall be very happy to confirm on oath if you find it necessary the following statement, as consisting with my belief and information. I recollect having conversed on the subject with you at Spottes, & soon after I spoke of it to my mother who is still alive, and who coincided with me in every particular.

My father came to Dunkillerick to herd it, at Whitsunday 1775, for, as I believe, Alexander Laidlaw in Clatteranshaws. My father left it at Whitsunday 1789, when I was nearly 14 years of age. I often, like other boys, in that state of life, assisted in herding, and used to run from home to Loch Grenoch and from one border of the farm to the other. It was perfectly well known I never contested that the <u>Waterfall</u> of the hill, that is the ridge on each side of which the rain when fallen runs in a particular

A letter in Murray's handwriting to James Stewart of Cairnsmore.
Courtesy of the Cairnsmore Archive

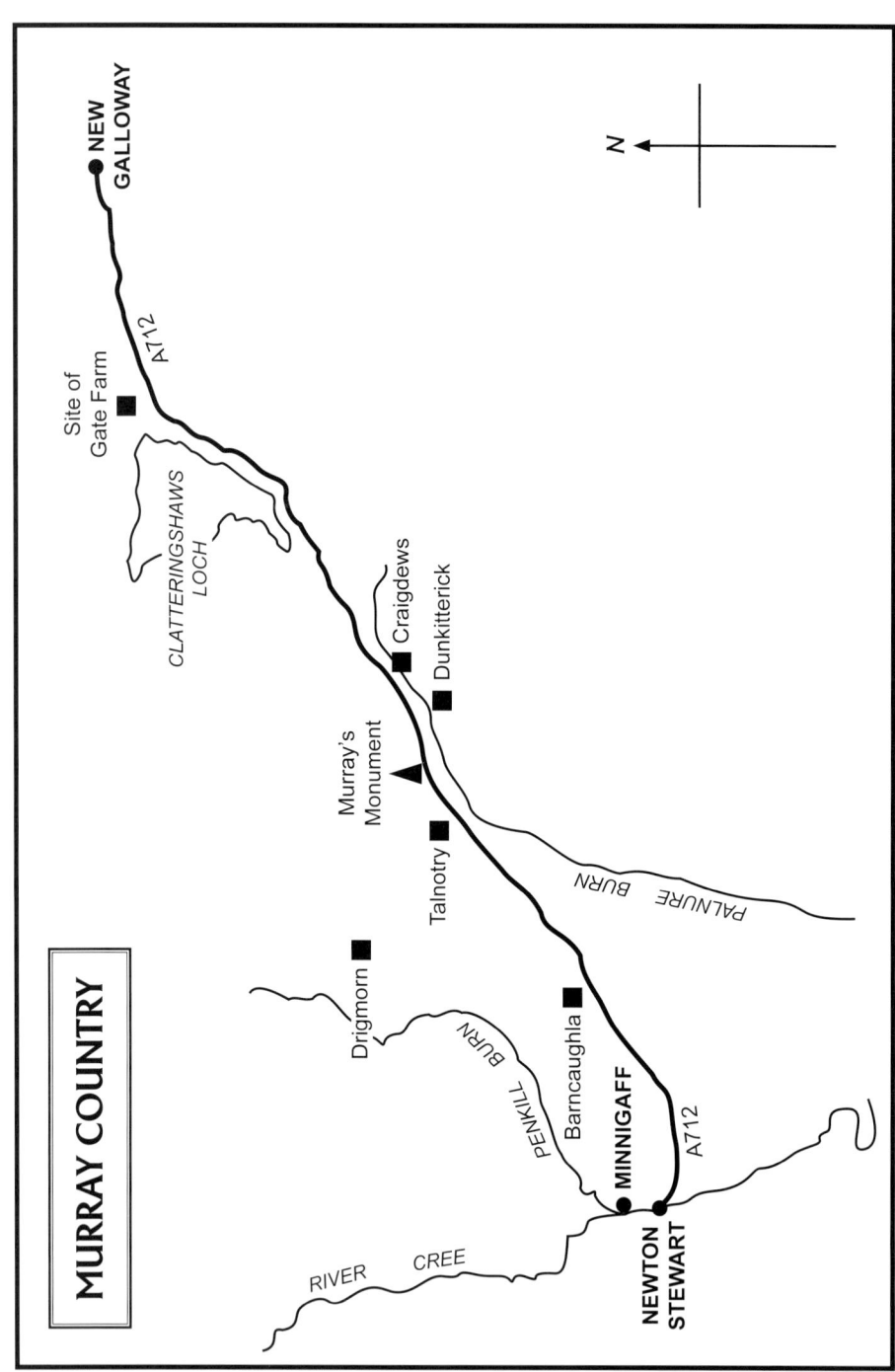

LIFE OF ALEXANDER MURRAY

1775	Born at (Dun)Kitterick to shepherd Robt Murray and second wife Mary Cochrane.
1781	Taught alphabet by father, enabling him to read omnivorously and write.
1784	Attended New Galloway school May-Nov. Left because of illness.
1785-9	Shepherd with father then resident tutor to children of local families.
1789	Family moved to Drigmorn. M able to attend Minnigaff school irregularly while still tutoring.
1790	Family moved to Barncaughla. M able to attend school more regularly. Continued tutoring.
1792	Left school. Often stayed in Newton Stewart with schoolfriend Jas McHarg.
1793	Unsuccessful application for Mochrum headmastership. Met Burns in Dumfries. Accepted for Edinburgh University.
1793-1802	Arts course then divinity course. Private tutoring. Wrote for and edited magazines and periodicals. Licensed to preach by presbytery of Edinburgh.
1802-5	Edited critically acclaimed edition of Bruce's *Travels to discover the Source of the Nile*.
1806	Appointed assistant minister to parish of Urr in the Stewartry.
1808	Chosen as minister of Urr. Married Henrietta Affleck of Grange Farm.
1812	Elected Professor of Oriental Languages at Edinburgh Univ.
1813	Died April 15th halfway through first session.

INTRODUCTION

Murray's Monument on the A712 from Newton Stewart to New Galloway is probably much better known than the man it commemorates. Thus the monument is listed in the index of C.H. Dick's magisterial *Highways and Byways in Galloway and Carrick* but not the man. Murray is indeed mentioned in several local books but is usually accorded a brief cliché reference as the shepherd boy who became a professor. He does scramble into *Highways and Byways* but only by way of a footnote. Similarly in *Discovering Galloway* he gains admission on the coat tails of a reference to his monument as one of the places of interest on that stretch of the A712. This treatment fails to do justice to the greatest linguist of his day. The present work is an attempt to allocate Alexander Murray his rightful place in the pantheon of Scottish geniuses by making clear the formidable difficulties he had to surmount in his brief career and the astonishing achievements he nevertheless accomplished.

In concentrating on those features, the book eschews any attempt at formal, chronological biography. However to give a context to the topics dealt with a synopsis of his life is given at the start in tabular form.

OBSTACLES

Alexander Murray had four major obstacles to overcome on his route to success. Perhaps the greatest was his physical handicaps. His description of himself as a "weakly child" is borne out by the facts. When he started school at New Galloway in 1784 at the age of nine he had to give up after a short time because of bad health. Similarly when the family moved to the farm of Drigmorn four miles from Minnigaff in 1789 Murray was able to attend the school there but only in summer and for two or three days each week because he was not "in stout health". His letters as an adult are punctuated by references to ill health preventing him from working: for example in 1810 he wrote to his publisher, Constable, "My late indisposition has retarded my philological treatise". A major objection cited to his candidacy for the chair of Oriental Languages at Edinburgh in 1812 was his poor health. The fact that the family home, the thatched, two-room, shepherd's cottage at Dunkitterick, was deprived of sun for three months in winter by the surrounding hills would do little to improve young Alexander's physical condition. He also suffered from bad eyesight, being extremely short-sighted. This made him a very poor shepherd boy because he had great difficulty in locating not only the sheep but even the cattle.

A pair of Murray's spectacles and their durable case now in the Stewartry Museum at Kirkcudbright. *Courtesy of Dumfries and Galloway Museums*

In ruins by 1790, the cottage at Dunkitterick was partially rebuilt in 1975 by the Forestry Commission.
Courtesy of John Pickin.

Presumably according to type, the cottage would have had a thatched roof and consisted of two rooms, the further away, with the original fireplace, for the human occupants and the nearer for the four moorland cattle which constituted virtually Robert Murray's entire wealth. *Courtesy of John Pickin.*

The view from the rear of Dunkitterick shows how it is dominated on the north by the bulk of Craigdews Hill: "The black rocks of Craigdews were constantly in our sight," Murray records. *Courtesy of John Pickin*

Patrick Heron and his family at Craigdews Farm half-a-mile to the north-east were the Murrays' nearest neighbours. *Photo: S. Hunter*

Another major handicap to Murray's career was that the remote environment of Dunkitterick severely limited his opportunities for the stimulus of social contact. The cottage in Palnure Glen, eight miles from Newton Stewart and ten from New Galloway, seems isolated today but it was even more so in Murray's day for the Edinburgh road, predecessor of the A712, did not then follow its present line through the glen and close to Dunkitterick but ran some distance to the north so that very few travellers passed near the lonely cottage apart from smugglers, who appreciated the absence of other traffic. Certainly the boy had one half-sister and four half-brothers but they were much older than he was for his father, Robert, was sixty-nine when Alexander was born to the shepherd's second wife. Consequently three of the brothers by then lived away from home. He did have a full sister, Mary, but she was three years younger. And Murray was no recluse; he enjoyed male company of his own age but did not get it apart from his brief spell at New Galloway until he was fourteen, when the move to Drigmorn allowed him to attend Minnigaff school and make friends like James McHarg, Robert Kerr, and Robert Cooper. The first-named became a lifelong friend but it was Robert Cooper who elicited from Murray the memorable remark, "Cooper left the (Minnigaff) school and went to Glasgow University or Wigton school. I forget which." His account of his high-spirited doings while staying with McHarg at Newton Stewart reveals a whole new side to his personality.

Because of the remoteness of Dunkitterick, Murray's poor health, and his father's financial circumstances ("My father had no money," says his son simply) Alexander had minimal formal schooling. His father taught him the letters of the alphabet at the age of six, using the charred end of a stem of heather rescued from the fire to write them on the back of an old comb for carding wool, thereby enabling him to read and write. From then till his departure for Edinburgh at the age of eighteen, Murray had a total of only 57 weeks of fractured schooling, briefly at New Galloway but mostly at Minnigaff. The Minnigaff headmaster was well educated and well meaning but easygoing and with a weakness for alcohol, providing little by way of inspiration or example. Consequently Murray was by necessity largely self-educated. Self-education requires an ample supply of good learning materials but in those radio-, TV-, internet-free days the boy from Dunkitterick did not even have access to a library. As a result his learning materials consisted of what in that lonely area he could beg, borrow, or occasionally buy.

   The diversity of subject-matter and sources found in his learning materials is testimony to Murray's insatiable thirst for knowledge. Thus he borrowed a volume of Plutarch and a book of Burns's poems from a farmer in Glentrool whose children he tutored. From a lead miner at Palnure he had on loan a copy of the *Iliad* in both Greek and Latin and an early history of Scotland. He bought from an old man in Minnigaff a large, elderly, Latin dictionary for 1/6d. When Lord Daer, heir to the Earl of Selkirk and an enthusiastic road builder, was helping decide the new line for the Edinburgh road, he lost his map of the local area near Dunkitterick and the finder gave it to Murray. Particularly poignant was the gift from a relative of an old Hebrew lexicon previously owned by Murray's second cousin, the tragically improvident, New Galloway-born Robert Heron, literary multi-tasker. This arbitrary, largely random acquisition of materials meant that it was purely a matter of chance which languages he became familiar with. The exception was French, which he chose to study at Minnigaff school as he intended to become a merchant's clerk in the West Indies in a similar career move to Robert Burns.

   It was perhaps also a matter of chance that his chosen subject and great passion was to become philology, the study of the history of and similarities between languages. At the age of twelve he borrowed from a neighbour at nearby Talnotry a copy of Salmon's *Geographical Grammar*. It contained the Lord's Prayer in the languages of all the countries dealt with in the book. Did this awaken his interest in comparing languages? Murray records that he derived "immense benefit" from Salmon's volume and that he "admired and mused on" the different versions of the Lord's Prayer.

The fourth obstacle to Alexander Murray's ambitions did not manifest itself until he was interviewed for a place at Edinburgh University in 1793. His speech stammer and awkwardness in expressing himself created a poor initial impression and it required a letter from his parish minister, Rev. Maitland of Minnigaff, to reassure Principal Baird that "these disadvantages do no justice to his knowledge...but are on the surface only" and obtain for the young man a highly successful formal interview before three academics. The problem arose again when he was a candidate for the professorship at Edinburgh in 1812. His defects of speech allied to his unprepossessing appearance and fact he was from a rural parish led to his being seen in some quarters as an uncouth country cousin unfitted for the high office he sought. That may account for his narrow victory (by only two votes) in the election despite testimonials in his favour from luminaries like Professors Dugald Stewart and Kirkmabreck-born Thos Brown; founder and legendary editor of *The Edinburgh Review* Francis Jeffrey; and Sir Walter Scott himself.

Alexander Murray: "a little man with a distinct stoop in his gait. He had black hair and brown eyes, and wore spectacles almost constantly ... on the right side of his face was a dark-red flesh mark, extending from his ear to his nose, which disfigured him."
Courtesy of Alex Shaw

SILVER LININGS

One of the remarkable features of Alexander Murray's career was the way in which major obstacles proved to have compensations that worked greatly to his advantage. His father was a shepherd as were his paternal and maternal grandfathers; his four half-brothers had all been brought up to be herds. The same career was intended for Alexander but his poor eyesight meant, as we have seen, that he was a failure as a herd boy. At first his father thought his fifth son was simply lazy and careless but when the real cause of the boy's incompetence was discovered Robert Murray accepted that Alexander would have to follow some other occupation and allowed him to start tutoring the children of local families. The way to his vocation was open.

In the same way the deficiencies of the headmaster at Minnigaff, where Murray received most of his schooling, proved almost to be a blessing. When the youth first went to Minnigaff School, although he was fourteen and had considerable experience as a tutor, he had only had a few weeks' formal schooling. A more conventional, orthodox headmaster than Mr Cramond would therefore have put him in the youngest and lowest class to learn the basics and thus have killed his enthusiasm. Instead he was not put in a particular class ("fettered to a class" is his way of describing it) but was allowed to join whatever group was doing work that interested him and to read and study any books in the school he wished. For him it was the ideal way "to enlarge my mind and range of thought".

When the family moved to Barncaughla ("hill of the gates"), Murray was able to attend Minnigaff school, only two miles away, more regularly.
Photo: S. Hunter

MURRAY'S ACHIEVEMENTS

Despite the daunting obstacles confronting him Alexander Murray compiled an astonishing range of achievements in his short life; these were not confined to the field of philology, where he gained international fame.

Educational

Murray's remarkable educational record is most effectively summarised in a series of bullet points, to borrow a term from the world of computing.

*At the age of twelve and after less than four months' formal schooling he was employed to tutor the children of local farmers, the first of several such commissions.

*When wellwishers Rev. Maitland of Minnigaff and school friend-turned-merchant James McHarg obtained for him an interview for a place at Edinburgh University in 1793, Murray had a thorough knowledge of French, Latin, Hebrew, and German together with some knowledge of Arabic, Abyssinian, Welsh, and Anglo-Saxon. He was then aged eighteen.

*While at university following an arts and then a divinity course, he added to his linguistic repertoire all the remaining European languages, both ancient and modern, and a clutch of Eastern tongues including Sanskrit, Persian, and some Chinese.

*When Murray's name was put forward for the Edinburgh professorship in 1812, one of the three other candidates, Dr David Dickson of St Cuthbert's, Edinburgh, instantly withdrew, saying it would be dishonourable for him to attempt to prevent the best qualified man from getting the chair.

Perhaps the most remarkable evidence of his academic status among his contemporaries occurred in 1811. In that year a letter arrived at the Foreign Office for King George III from the governor of Tigre province in Abyssinia. It was written in the Tigre(Geez) dialect of Abyssinian. The Foreign Office sought advice in academic circles and was told that the only man in Britain who could translate the letter was Alexander Murray. The missive was dispatched post haste to the manse at Haugh of Urr, where Murray was parish minister, and a translation quickly forthcoming. The communication from Abyssinia was a thank-you letter for a shipment of weapons which the British government had sent to the governor, together with a strong hint that another shipment would not go amiss. Britain's involvement in the international arms trade has a long pedigree.

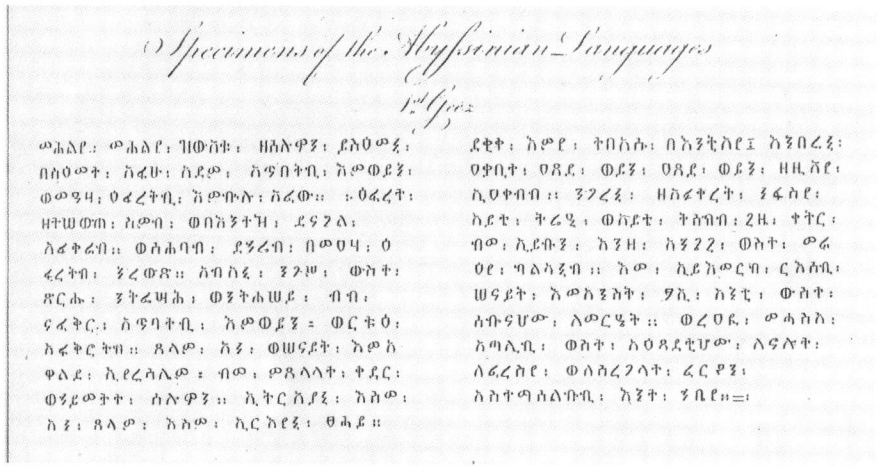

The Geez form of Abyssinian used in the governor's letter.
Courtesy of Dumfries and Galloway Libraries

Literary

The failed herd's fame in Scottish literary circles preceded his renown as a linguist. His interest in this sphere is hardly surprising because from an early age he was a great lover of literature, especially poetry, with a catholic taste which comprehended works in Scots, English, Greek, and Latin, including both official and popular works.

His favourites ranged from Milton's *Paradise Lost* by way of Homer, Ovid, Burns, and Sir David Lindsay to the ballad *Chevy Chase* and numerous other examples of both traditional and popular ballads. Unsurprisingly he started writing poetry at an early age. He wrote in both Scots and English on conventional, local subjects, for example *Verses to Craignelder* and *My Native Vale*. Encouraged by his friends, he considered publishing a volume of poetry and travelled to Dumfries to seek the opinion of Robert Burns. Burns advised against publication, suggesting that in later years Murray might regret these youthful effusions being in print. Perusal of a few lines from the latter poem makes it difficult to disagree with Burns's judgement:

"While Cree, from hills whose wide domain
 To Scotland's throne a Hero gave,
 Rolls her dark torrent to the main,
 To sink in Wigtown's distant wave;
 Her mountain stream my soul shall cheer
 While softer memories, still more dear,
 Waked by fair Fancy's kindling art,
 Shall beam in ardors round my heart."

Another very different literary project was initiated after Alexander's reading of the great classical epics. He decided that he too would write an epic, his chosen subject being Arthur, legendary king of the Britons. This time his unsophisticated Minnigaff friends were even more enthusiastic about the results but the poet himself realised it was mediocre stuff and abandoned the undertaking after completing seven of the statutory ten books, destroying the manuscript. Tantalisingly, he started to gather material for a history of Galloway but regrettably abandoned the idea.

Although Murray had poems and articles published in two prestigious periodicals, *The Scots Magazine* and *The Edinburgh Review*, his achievements as an author are interesting rather than important and contributed nothing to his reputation. It was far different with his work as an editor. For six months in 1802 at the conclusion of his divinity

ACCOUNT

OF THE

LIFE AND WRITINGS

OF

JAMES BRUCE, OF KINNAIRD, ESQ. F.R.S.

AUTHOR OF

TRAVELS TO DISCOVER

THE SOURCE OF THE NILE,

IN THE YEARS

1768, 1769, 1770, 1771, 1772, & 1773.

BY ALEXANDER MURRAY, F. A. S. E.
AND SECRETARY FOR FOREIGN CORRESPONDENCE.

EDINBURGH:

Printed by George Ramsay and Company,
FOR ARCHIBALD CONSTABLE AND COMPANY, AND MANNERS AND MILLER, EDINBURGH;
AND LONGMAN, HURST, REES, AND ORME, LONDON.

1808.

Murray wrote a biography of James Bruce as a companion volume to his edition of the explorer's *Travels… Courtesy of Dumfries and Galloway Libraries*

course he edited *The Scots Magazine,* not the modern D.C. Thomson version, an unfailingly interesting and enjoyable leisure read, but the original heavyweight periodical, which like today's *Sunday Herald* would have claimed to be "Scotland's News Magazine". Having cut his editorial teeth on that, he was invited by its publisher, Constable, to undertake the editing of a second edition of one of the most celebrated works of the time, *Travels to Discover the Source of the Nile* by the Scottish explorer James Bruce. Since most of the travels had taken place in Abyssinia and Murray knew all of that country's five dialects, he seemed an ideal choice. And so it proved. He was able to use Bruce's archive, including documents in their original language, to produce a greatly expanded and much more accurate edition of the famous book. It took three years to complete, ran to seven volumes, won great praise, and made Murray's name in the academic world.

Ecclesiastical

In 1806 the former divinity student, now a licensed preacher, was appointed assistant minister in the parish of Urr in the Stewartry. Two years later he became minister at Urr, a position he held until his death in 1813. The new assistant owed his appointment to the good offices of a local landowner William Douglas of Orchardton, the nephew of the developer of Newton Stewart and founder of Castle Douglas. Nephew William had received language tutoring in Edinburgh from Murray preparatory to visiting the Eastern Mediterranean. During the latter's assistantship he stayed with his maternal uncle William Cochrane, the man who had financed his first session at school, in New Galloway, in 1784 but who had now given up the Scots drapery trade in England for farming at Grange in the Urr valley.

Murray's ministerial career was solid rather than spectacular but it is important to stress one fact. This was a time when young men of scholarly disposition often sought a career in the ministry not for spiritual reasons but because it gave them time for academic study and research. Murray did plenty of both at Urr but he had a genuine sense

Grandfather clock which belonged to William Cochrane, Murray's maternal uncle, who financed the boy's attendance at Kells school in New Galloway. The round disc above the face bears the inscription "William and Ann Cochrane".
Courtesy of Alex Shaw

of vocation. He was a good preacher, always without written version or notes, although the claim of a correspondent in the *Dumfries and Galloway Courier* that "his discourses were animated and sublime" seems a trifle exaggerated. (Murray himself said that his sermons were popular because they were lengthy enough, sometimes over three hours, to meet the expectations of his congregation: "I preach as long as they please".) In his pastoral duties he was conscientious and diligent; the claim by the *Courier* correspondent that he was "beloved of his flock as a father and a friend" this time seems readily credible. In a farewell letter to one of his elders Murray explained he had taken the professorial post only because his health made him unable to carry out his duties in a far flung parish according to his standards.

As a minister he had decidedly liberal views. On the great political issue of the day, Catholic Emancipation, he felt that Irish Catholics should have their religious and political liberties restored and enjoy equal treatment with Protestants. His educational ideas were well ahead of his time: forty years before the introduction of compulsory, state-financed education he advocated that the children of the poor ought to be educated, an opinion which few of his contemporaries would have endorsed.

Philological

However, the achievement which admitted Alexander Murray to the select circle of Scottish men of genius was in the field of comparative philology, the study of the history of and similarities between languages. Arguably the most important discovery that has been made in European language study is that all European languages, bar four, together with a substantial number of those of the Near East belong to the same family, being descended from a common ancestor, a hypothetical language given the name Indo-European. Credit for the discovery of Indo-European is conventionally awarded to two German researchers, Bopp and Grimm, who separately enunciated the theory in works published in 1816 and 1819 respectively. Murray also stated

HISTORY

OF THE

EUROPEAN LANGUAGES;

OR,

RESEARCHES INTO THE AFFINITIES
OF THE TEUTONIC, GREEK, CELTIC, SCLAVONIC,
AND INDIAN NATIONS.

BY THE LATE

ALEXANDER MURRAY, D.D.

PROFESSOR OF ORIENTAL LANGUAGES IN THE UNIVERSITY OF
EDINBURGH.

WITH

A LIFE OF THE AUTHOR.

VOL. I.

EDINBURGH:
PRINTED FOR ARCHIBALD CONSTABLE & CO. EDINBURGH;
AND HURST, ROBINSON, AND CO. LONDON.

1823.

Title page of Murray's great work *History of the European Languages*.
Courtesy of Dumfries and Galloway Libraries

the Indo-European theory at length and in detail in his book *History of the European Languages* as the sub-title makes clear: *Researches into the Affinities of the Teutonic, Greek, Celtic, Sclavonic, and Indian Nations*. However Murray's two-volume work was not published until 1823, seven years after Bopp announced his discovery, and so he received no credit. But Murray's book was finished by 1812 although his appointment to the professorship and need to prepare lectures for his first session left no time to arrange its publication. His death in 1813 ended any hope of his final work going through the press at that time. And so Alexander Murray's greatest achievement, the discovery of Indo-European, and position as the founder of the science of comparative philology go unhonoured and unsung.

Yet there is no doubt about the validity of both claims. In a prospectus which appeared in an edition of his life of "Abyssinian" Bruce in 1808, Murray wrote: "Greek and Latin are only dialects of a language much more simple, regular, and ancient which forms the basis of almost all the tongues of Europe and … of Sanskrit itself. This opinion is founded on actual observation and analysis". And a letter to Principal Baird of Edinburgh University written in 1810, six years before Bopp published his work, gives an example of that observation and analysis: "It will amuse you to hear that *oeda* in Icelandic and *veda* in Sanskrit are not only in the main the same word but are actually the same as our own term *wit* or *wita* – knowledge."

In his philological studies, once again in Murray's life an obstacle, this time the lack of study materials, had turned into an advantage. He rarely had a grammar or textbook to help him learn a language but usually a dictionary or alphabet along with a familiar book or text like the New Testament or the Lord's Prayer. His consequent concentration on the vocabulary of a language rather than the grammar or syntax led him to see the similarities among languages for it is in the vocabulary that the common elements are found and not in the grammar or syntax. These latter are arguably the reflection of the national character of the users of the language and so are dissimilar from one tongue to another.

(The famous Glasgow form of the imperative mood: "Gonnae no dae that" is a good example at dialect, regional level.) Thus people learning a language in the conventional way, studying grammar, syntax, and vocabulary simultaneously, are less likely to see the elements shared by languages than Murray, the latter using what he describes as "the method dictated by necessity in the absence of all assistance."

THE LAST CHAPTER

Old Quad, Edinburgh University. *Photo: F. Hunter*

With his election to Edinburgh University's Chair of Oriental Languages (also known in the groves of academe as the Hebrew Professorship) Alexander Murray had reached the pinnacle of the academic world but his time there was brutally short. He began his lectures in October, 1912, but his chronic ill health, caused by asthma and underlying consumption (tuberculosis), worsened and by early 1813 he was seriously ill. He died in April of that year, a bout of pneumonia administering the coup de grace. He left behind a wife, daughter, and son. By a tragic coincidence the first two also died of tuberculosis while his son was drowned on his first voyage as a ship's doctor when his vessel, the merchant ship *Elizabeth*, was wrecked off the coast of Canada while bound for Quebec.

However at least one human link between the linguist and his native Galloway survives in the person of a descendant of Murray's full sister Mary, who married a neighbour called Alexander Shaw from Gate Farm just east of today's Clatteringshaws Loch, a 1930's hydroelectric creation. (The Shaw family has been in the Glenkens for over 400 years.) Also a descendant in an earlier generation of that marriage was the legendary Provost Ebenezer Shaw, holder of three university degrees, student friend of R. L. Stevenson and Arthur Conan Doyle, and dominant figure in the public life of the town and county of Wigtown in the 1920's and 1930's. Thus was strengthened the connection between Murray and Wigtown created when he was eighteen and was introduced to the Rev. Duncan, the parish minister, "an excellent man and a scholar", who encouraged him and loaned him books.

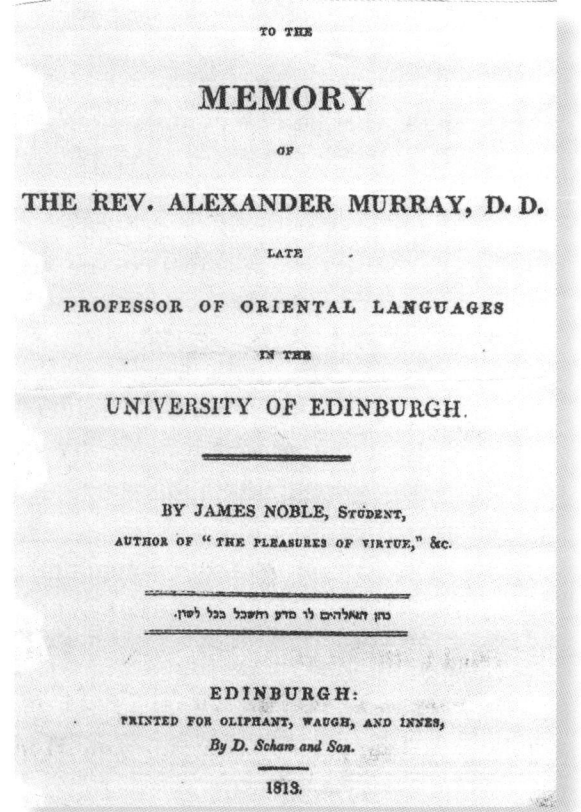

Poetic evidence of the esteem in which Murray was held by his students despite his brief tenure of office.
Courtesy of Douglas McDavid

Harvesting timber on the Gate Flow (peat bog) east of Clatteringshaws Loch has revealed former fields and dykes on Gate Farm, home of Murray's sister and brother-in-law. *Photo: S. Hunter*

Ebenezer Shaw, dominant figure in the public life of 1920's and 1930's Wigtown and friend of famous authors, was a descendant of Alexander Murray.
Courtesy of Dumfries and Galloway Libraries

"FROM YON LONE HEIGHT A TOWER LOOKS DOWN"

In 1834 over twenty years after Alexander Murray's death a campaign was initiated to raise funds for a monument to him. The moving spirit behind it was James Stewart, laird of Cairnsmore, on whose 8,000-acre estate Dunkitterick stood. The shepherd's cottage had been in ruins before 1800 but the low-lying location frowned upon by the surrounding hills seemed an undesirably inconspicuous choice for the memorial. The site eventually selected was Duncraig Hill, then known as Doon Hill, close to Murray's birthplace and even closer to the Grey Mare's Tail waterfall. Both versions of the name indicate by the first syllable that an Iron Age fort once stood on the spot selected.

James Stewart of Cairnsmore, whose "exertions and skill" (in the words of the inscription) were mainly responsible for the creation of Murray's Monument.
Courtesy of Mrs N. Champion

The location seems ideal: the monument can be seen, courtesy of the ice-carved valley of the Palnure Burn, from the clachan of Longcastle in the Machars between Whauphill and Port William sixteen miles away as the crow flies:

"............................From yon lone height
A tower looks down the long, wide lane of light
That leads to distant Solway".

To the east an extended straight on the A712 acts as an avenue leading to it. It comes as a surprise therefore to learn from Stewart family tradition that this was the second-choice site although the first choice is unknown. However a letter from the tenant farmer of Talnotry, John McCallan, to laird James Stewart may furnish a clue. In the missive McCallan formally waives all right to compensation for damage to his land caused by erecting the monument or transporting materials to it provided that the monument is built on "the Doon rock" on his farm. It seems that the original site chosen had not been to his liking and may have been on land he tenanted.

The fund-raising campaign elicited a wide geographical and social response ranging from local farmers by way of The Keeper of the Scottish Records, the headmaster of Edinburgh's Royal High School together with sundry professors, advocates, and lawyers, to the Church of Scotland ministers of Rotterdam and Bombay. Nevertheless it was only a partial success, leaving a shortfall of seventy pounds from the contract price for erecting the monument. Once again James Stewart played a vital role. Having contributed to the fund and donated the ground for the monument, he now offered a loan of the necessary seventy pounds. The offer was gratefully accepted and it is doubtful if the money was repaid in spite of a second public appeal. The obelisk did not acquire an inscription till many years later.

It appears from his correspondence that the ubiquitous James Stewart also had a role in designing the proposed memorial. Preliminary sketches for a more ornate structure having been rejected as unsuitable for the surroundings, the final version was a pillar of local granite 80

> Cretown, 9th May 1824
>
> We give this as our estimate at the sum of £283.16.9 for erecting the Monument on the Doon hill in the Parish of Minigaff according to the plan and specifications shewn, with the exceptions of the polished stone for the Inscription, and with the consideration of getting the stones on Craigjews for the outside of the Building, and them for the inside where they can be found most suitable.
>
> James Darguvel
> David Shaw

The successful tender for the construction of the monument.
Courtesy of the Cairnsmore Archive

> Estimate
>
> I do hereby offer to finish the Monument proposed to be built upon the Farm of Talnotrie agreeable to plan and Specifications for the Sum of £315 Sto
>
> A. Sibbald

A. Sibbald's unsuccessful estimate puzzles by its offer to "finish" a monument "proposed to be built". *Courtesy of the Cairnsmore Archive*

feet high. The successful tender was for material for the walls to come from Craigdews nearly two miles away but Stewart family tradition says the stone came from Talnotry in the immediate vicinity. For the hollow interior the stones for the rubble infill or hearting were to be obtained "where they can be found most suitably" presumably from the surrounding hillsides. The contract to build the monument was awarded to the Creetown-based firm of James Dargavel and David Shaw, their successful tender of £283.16.9 excluding the polished stone for the inscription. A change of contractor seems to have taken place halfway through the work for in June and July, 1835, the monthly payments of twenty to fifty pounds were made to the Creetown firm but for August and September the recipient was one James McNab although he had not been one of the original tenderers . Whatever the identity of the builders, the work was personally supervised by James Stewart, who left his home at Cairnsmore House at six every morning for that purpose.

Despite the twenty-one years that had passed since Murray's death the laying of the foundation stone in June, 1834, was watched by an estimated crowd of 3,000 people, tribute to the enduring esteem in which he was held. The occasion was a splendid one, attended by three bands and representatives of seven Masonic lodges, of which body the late professor was presumably a member. In the absence through illness of Viscount Kenmure the ceremony was performed by the Provincial Grand Master. The construction was finished by November, 1835, but another 42 years were to pass before the undertaking was finally completed by the addition of the inscription. By that time the monument was only 70 feet high: a lightning strike had damaged the top and the affected portion was removed. In compensation the stable door was firmly secured by the addition of a lightning conductor.

The year 1877 saw not only the long-delayed addition of the dedication to the monument on Duncraig but also the erection of another tribute to Galloway's linguistic genius. The site this time was Murray's grave in the churchyard of historic Greyfriars church in the

Although both the location and the design of Murray's Monument were second choices, the result is impressive. *Courtesy of John Pickin*

The monument from the south-west before the landscape was smothered by conifers. Talnotry Farm, of which no trace remains, is in the right foreground.

heart of Edinburgh and the parties responsible were, in the words of the inscription, "admirers chiefly connected with Galloway". Given the timing it seems likely that the same benefactors were responsible for the belated lettering on the Duncraig memorial. The seventeen-feet-high obelisk at Greyfriars occupies an appropriately prominent position close to the north-west corner of the church in a place than which no other location has stronger links with the Covenanting movement of the seventeenth century, a crucial chapter in the story of the Church of Scotland. Equally appropriate was the choice of Dalbeattie granite for the building material as the quarries are just over the parish boundary from Urr, Murray's only pastoral charge.

As for the linguist's birthplace, the cottage at Dunkitterick, abandoned and in ruins twenty years before he died, was almost obliterated by military exercises during the Second World War. However the walls were partly restored in 1975 by the Forestry Commission, complementing the monument on nearby Duncraig.

The Edinburgh memorial may languish in undeserved obscurity and the inconspicuous shell of the house at Dunkitterick be largely ignored by passing travellers but high-profile Murray's Monument in the Galloway hills is known at least by sight to hundreds, perhaps thousands, of people. Two hundred years after his death it is surely time that the man himself and his extraordinary achievements should enjoy equal recognition.

The inscription was added forty-two years after the monument was erected.
Courtesy of John Pickin

The memorial over Alexander Murray's grave in Edinburgh's Greyfriars churchyard.
Photo: F. Hunter

The view from Murray's Monument north-east up the valley of the Palnure Burn. Dunkitterick, three-quarters of a mile away, is hidden from view by the conifers but its position indicated by the arrowhead of cleared land in the right background. The bulk of Craigdews Hill on the left is prominent with the Old Edinburgh Road, the highway in Murray's day, out of sight to the north of it. *Courtesy of John Pickin*

SOURCES

Bonner, A.	*Alexander Murray* ....*Galloway Gazette* 1974
Brown, J.F.	*From Shepherd's Cot to Professor's Chair: Centenary Celebrations in Commemoration of Alexander Murray D.D.* ....*Galloway Gazette* 1913
Champion, Mrs N.	personal communication
Dick, C.H.	*Highways and Byways in Galloway and Carrick* ....Macmillan 1916
McCormick, A.	*Galloway: The Spell of Its Hills and Glens* ....Smith 1947
McDavid, D.	personal communication
Macleod, I.	*Discovering Galloway* ....Donald 1986
Murray, T.	*The Literary History of Galloway 2nd edn* ...... Waugh & Innes 1832
Pate, Mrs L.	personal communication
Reith, J	*The Life and Writings of Rev. Alex. Murray* .... Maxwell 1903
Shaw, Alex.	personal communication

The Cairnsmore Archive ....(unpublished)

Dumfries and Galloway Courier,...... issue of 20th April, 1813.

ACKNOWLEDGEMENTS

This publication is an expanded version of a talk given at the 2013 Wigtown Book Festival. That talk was the result of the untiring efforts made by Mrs Sheila Laird of Glenlochar near Castle Douglas to ensure that the bicentenary of Alexander Murray's death was adequately commemorated. I readily acknowledge her key role in the genesis of this work. Mrs Laird put me in touch with Mr Alex Shaw of Balmaclellan, a descendant of Murray, who was generous in his provision of information about the family's history. I owe a huge debt of gratitude to Mr and Mrs Champion of Cairnsmore House, who offered the resources of the Cairnsmore Archive of previously unpublished material, and to archivist Frances Wilkins, who facilitated access to it. Staff members, past and present, of Dumfries and Galloway Libraries' and Museums' Services provided willing assistance.

However all factual errors, suppositions, assumptions, and speculations are my sole responsibility.

Except where otherwise attributed, the quotations by Alexander Murray are taken from a "memoir" he wrote for Rev Maitland, minister of Minnigaff, in July, 1812, a fortnight after his election as professor. Maitland had been asked by Principal Baird of Edinburgh University to obtain details of Murray's life before he enrolled at Edinburgh in 1794 and decided to get them from the horse's mouth. Murray reluctantly ("I have as yet done nothing that…entitles me to a place in the most trivial volume of Biography") but comprehensively agreed. The quotations are taken from an unabridged copy of the memoir in the Cairnsmore Archive.

The lines quoted on Page 14 are from a poem by C.S. Dougall, headmaster of the Ewart High School, Newton Stewart, around 1900.

Previous Trust Publications

Stranraer in World War Two	— Archie Bell
The Loss of the Princess Victoria	— Jack Hunter
The Cairnryan Military Railway *	— Bill Gill
A Peep at Stranraer's Past *	— Donnie Nelson
Royal Burgh of Stranraer 1617 — 2000	— J.S. Boyd
	— Jack Hunter
	— Donnie Nelson
	— Christine Wilson
Don't Plague the Ferryman *	— Trevor Boult
Portpatrick to Donaghadee *	— Fraser G. MacHaffie
The Rhins Forgotten Air Disaster *	— Sandy Rankin
Place-names in the Rhinns of Galloway *	— Prof. John MacQueen
Auld Lang Syne in the Rhins of Galloway	— Prof. Charles McNeil
The Lost Town of Innermessan *	— Jack Hunter
Every Beach a Port *	— Bill McCormack
Aircrew in Wartime	— Norman Fidler
Prehistoric Settlement in the Wigtownshire Moors	— Dr. Jane Murray
100 Years of Stranraer Golf Club	— James Blair
	— Andrew Hannay
	— James Sproule
Garlieston — Emergence of a Village *	— David Kirkwood
A Flight Too Far	— Jack Hunter
Place-names of the Wigtownshire Moors and Machars	— Prof. John MacQueen
The Wigtownshire Constabulary	— David Kirkwood
Wigtownshire Vernacular Buildings	— John R. Hume
Bobbies on the Beat	— David Kirkwood
The Parish Of Kirkmaiden 1854	— William Todd
A Galloway Man Among "The Few"	— Jack Hunter
The Friendly Invaders *	— Jack Hunter
	— Tom McCreath
	— John Scoular
Wait Till Your Father Comes Home on Leave	— Donnie Nelson
Glasgow's Galloway School	— David Kirkwood
The Earls of Galloway and Galloway House	— David Kirkwood

Out of print

Stranraer and District Local History Trust Membership 2013 - 2014

Mr John Adams
Mrs Muriel Adams
Mrs Sheelagh Afia
Mr Peter Armitage
Mr David Baird
Mrs Elaine Barton,
   Vice Chairman
Mr A. J. Beattie
Mrs Betty Beck
Mr Archie Bell — Author
Mrs Dorothy Bell
Mr Trevor Boult — Author
Mr Douglas Brown
Mrs H. G. Brown
Mr David B. Cairns
Mr Adam Calderwood
Mr John Cameron
Mrs Pat Cameron
Mr John Carruth
Mr Iain Clark
Mrs Janet Clark
Mrs Maureen Clark
Comm. Keith Cochrane
Mr J M Colledge
Mrs Harriet Collins
Mrs Marion Cunningham
Mr J. P. Davis
Lord Dervaird
Mr G. E. Dickson-Hamilton
Mr Bill Dougan
Mr J. J. S. Farmer
Mr Jim Ferguson
Mr Norman Fidler
   — Author
Mr C. J. Findlay
Ms Rosemary Gall
Mrs Agnes Goddard
Miss D. Gorman
Mrs Irene Grant
Mrs G. O. Gray
Mr Iain Gray
Mrs Janette Hall
Mrs M. J. Heaney
Mr W. A. Heaney
Mr John Hume — Author
Mr Jack Hunter — Author
Mr David Iredale
Mr Ronnie Irving
Mr Hugh Jaques
Mrs E. A. Jenkins
Mr David Kirkwood
   — Author
Mr P. H. K. Lilley
Mrs Margaret MacArthur
Mrs Rosemary McCormack
Mr Tom McCreath
   — Author
Mr G McCredie
Mr Colin McCubbin
Mrs J. C. MacDonald
Mr Michael McDowall
Prof. Alastair McGowan
Mrs M W McGowan
Prof. Fraser McHaffie
   — Author
Mr Donald McHarrie
Mrs Nancy McLucas
Prof. John MacQueen
   — Author
Mrs Winifred MacQueen
Mr Robert Malcolm
Mrs Patricia Martin
Mr Harry Monteith
Mr Alasdair Morgan
Dr Jane Murray — Author
Mr Donnie Nelson,
   Chairman — Author
Mrs Mae Nelson
Mrs Helen Nish
Mrs Elizabeth Pate
Mr Robert Pate
Mr Alan Peace
Mr John Pickin
Mr Jim Pratt
Mrs Margaret Pratt
Mr Jim Rafferty
Mr Sandy Rankin — Author
Ms Maria Roy
Mrs Helen Scott
Mr John Scoular — Author
Mr P. N. Skinner
Dr E. A. W. Slater
Mrs Jane Sloan
Mr Brian Smith
Mrs Renee Smith
Mr James Sproule — Author
Mr D. J. Start
Mr Tom Stevenson,
   Hon. Treasurer
Mrs Sheila Stevenson
Mr A. C. Thompson
Mr C. R. A. Tucker
Mr Barry Unwin
Mr Russell Walker
Mr Owen Watt
Mr David Williamson
Mrs Christine Wilson,
   Hon. Secy. — Author
Mr Eric Wilson
Mrs Elizabeth Wilson
Mr William Wilson

Stranraer and District Local History Trust was constituted in 1998 at the instigation of Stranraer and District Chamber of Commerce. All work of the Trust, including author's work preparation and editing of our books for printing, recording of memories and production of CDs is executed by our volunteer members

Membership for 2014—2015 is £4
This entitles members to a discount of 20% on copies of publications when purchased from the Secretary.

Books can be ordered by mail with cheque made out to Stranraer and District Local History Trust, postage to be included, from the Hon. Secretary, Christine Wilson,
Tall Trees,
London Road,
Stranraer,
DG9 8BZ
or on the website
www.stranraerhistory.org.uk
We maintain a web-site where up to date information about the Trust may be obtained